A Religion of Books

A Religion of Books

God's Tools in the History of Salvation

KLAUS BOCKMUEHL

COMMUNITY CHRISTIAN MINISTRIES
MOSCOW, IDAHO

(First in a series of monographs by Regent College)

Special Edition 2020 by Community Christian Ministries
P.O. Box 9754, Moscow, Idaho 83843 (208) 883-0997

Reprinted by permission of
Regent College and Helmers & Howard, Publishers Inc.

First Edition 1986 by Regent College
2130 Wesbrook Mall, Vancouver, B.C., Canada V6T1W6

Helmers & Howard, Publishers Inc.
1221 East Madison Street, Colorado Springs, Colorado 80907, USA
Translation of *Bücher, wozu?*
Includes bibliographical references.
ISBN 978-1-8828-4035-9
1. Christian literature — Publication and distribution.
2. Books — History. I. Title.
BV2369. B6613 1985 070.5'09 C85-091410-8

© Klaus Bockmuehl
Printed first by Brunnen Verlag, Giessen, West Germany.

20 21 22 23 24 25 26 27 28   9 8 7 6 5 4 3 2 1

Contents

Preface	1
About the Author	3
Some Historical Data	7
Books and Readers in Scripture	7
Books—God's Tools in History	14
Excursion: The Role of Literature in the Political Revolutions of Modern History	51
Present-Day Opportunities	63
The Future of Books	63
Ways and Means of Christian Work with Books	74
Aim and Purpose of Christian Literature Work	95

Preface

Books are life-changing, for good or bad. Very few books have a neutral effect on the reader. Of those that do, very few of those few would stay in print.

It was about three years after my conversion to Christ that I found out that there was such a thing as a Christian book. About the same time, I discovered there were Christian bookstores. The Biola Bookstore in Kowloon, Hong Kong, was the first such bookstore I entered. That was in March 1951. It was then that I became a reader of Christian books and a distributor of books and booklets to believers and unbelievers.

In the nearly seventy years since that time, I have been greatly impressed with two things: the life-changing power of the Gospel in print and the fact that relatively few Christians will give a book to an unbeliever, even if they received Christ reading that particular book.

In the early 1990s, I came across this little book by Klaus Bockmuehl. I was impressed with three things: the title, the content, and the author. (My wife, Bessie, and I had audited a class he taught at Regent College in the fall of 1979.) We immediately bought all remaining copies of it!

We are grateful to Elisabeth Bockmuehl and Helmers and Howard, Publishers Inc. for permission to reprint this little book.

JIM WILSON
Moscow, Idaho
2020

About the Author

My husband, Klaus Bockmuehl, was 58 years old when he died in 1989 after struggling with cancer for four years. During the last eight months of his life, he started and completed his last book, *Listening to the God Who Speaks* (Helmers & Howard). Until the very last day, Klaus would talk about his thankfulness to God and about wanting to use every day "to strengthen the brethren" and to "hold Jesus dear."

Klaus was born in the industrial town of Essen in Germany. He became a Christian in the inner-city youth ministry led by Pastor

W. Busch, who gave Klaus his roots in German Pietism. While he was growing up, Klaus intended to become a chemical engineer. But when he visited the conference centre of Moral Rearmament in Caux, Switzerland, in 1948, he felt called to study theology. Klaus studied theology, philosophy, and sociology in Tubingen, Gottingen, London and Basel, and he finished his Ph.D. in 1959 with a thesis on the critique of religion and the anthropology of Karl Marx.

We were married in 1961. Our three children were born within the first five years of our marriage. During this time, Klaus worked as a pastor. From 1971 to 1977, we lived in Basel, where Klaus taught at the theological seminary St. Chrischona.

In 1977 Klaus was asked to join the faculty of Regent College in Vancouver, British Columbia, as Professor of Theology and Ethics. This was not an easy move for us to take, but gradually we all came to love Canada, Vancouver, and Regent College. A great help in all the upheaval was that one by one our children found their own genuine commitment to the Lord, which was and is a reason of deep thankfulness.

Although working in North America, Klaus remained a strong voice in the German-speaking evangelical world, especially against the secularization of theology. In his publications, he criticized ethical relativism, and he pleaded for a rediscovery of the Holy Spirit in ethics. Klaus was convinced that personal renewal and social responsibility should go hand in hand. For him, this was the message of the double commandment of love.

Klaus' theological work was almost exclusively the fruit of his spirituality. He started every day with an early time of quiet and prayer, and most of his ideas and inspirations were given to him during these hours every morning. His daily devotions were centered on Scripture, and this was the secret of his integrity, humility, and teaching.

One month before he died, Klaus gave the convocation address to the graduating class of Regent College from his wheelchair. I end this little introduction with a quote from this address: "If there is one faculty we need to have for the next phase in life, it is not the sharp teeth and swift legs needed for the 'rat race,' but the listening heart for which King Solomon asked when he was granted a wish from God."

ELISABETH BOCKMUEHL
Vancouver
June 17, 1992

Some Historical Data

Books and Readers in Scripture

In praise of books it has been said: "Without books, God would be silent..." Now we all know that is not true. It is an exaggeration. God spoke to the prophets, He spoke to us in the person of His own Son, in each case before the respective book came into being. Nevertheless, the Christian faith has indeed repeatedly been called a "religion of the book." This is literally true, for our word "Bible" originates from the Greek and means nothing but "the book." The Bible is the book *per se*, and the Bible sets the standard for the Christian faith.

Apart from the incarnation of His Son and next to oral preaching, God has chosen the medium of the book in order to proclaim His goodness to us. In a conspicuous manner, the book has become a prominent tool for God's plan of salvation with the world.

The fact that God laid a book into the hands of mankind caused Johann Georg Hamann, the eminent Christian philosopher of the Enlightenment era, to exclaim 200 years ago, "Just imagine—God a writer!" Hamann meant to say: what a remarkable condescendence of God, that he should make himself equal to the species of human writers!

Behind this remark obviously lies an existential knowledge of the flimsy place and prestige of authors in society generally. God has, as it were, let himself become one of them. For God, the book is not much better than the manger: a humble appearance hiding a treasure.

Books are already mentioned in Scripture itself. It turns out that even with God in Heaven there exist a number of "books." Thus the Bible mentions the fact that God keeps a "Book of Life." Moses says, "If you will not forgive the sins of your people once again, then blot me out of your book which you have written!" (Ex. 32:32). Jesus praises His disciples, "Rejoice, for your names are written in Heaven!" (Lk. 10:20) and thus indicates how eternally important it is for every person whether his name is known by God or not (cf. also Ps. 69:28; Dan. 12:1; Phil. 4:3; Rev. 3:5, 17:8).

However, there is not only the Book of Life, but there are also the Books of Judgment. God is keeping books about mankind. In Revelation we read, "And the books were opened, and the dead judged according to what was written about them in the books, according to their works" (Rev. 20:12, cf. Dan. 7:10).

The third thing which we hear about books in the hand of God is that there exists a Book of Providence, a written plan of salvation, a book which contains God's intentions for the history of the world. Psalm 139:16 says, "All the days were written onto your book." Another passage talks about the coming Messiah: "Behold, I am coming; in the book it is written of me" (Ps. 40:7). The Book of Providence contains all that is to come. For human beings it is a "book with seven seals" (Rev. 5:1); only Christ is able to open and read it.

On the other hand, there are those books which according to the Bible are given into the hands of man. First of all, there is the "Book of Covenant," the document of God's covenant with Israel. "Moses took the Book of Covenant and read from it" (Ex. 24:7).

Apart from this basic book of the law, other books are also mentioned. For instance, one man sighs, "Oh that my words were written in a book!" (Job 19:23). Some prophets receive God's explicit order to put into writing all the instructions they obtained: "Write in a book all the words which I have spoken to you!" (Jer. 36:2, 4, 28; cf. Is. 8:1, 30:8; Hab. 2:2).

Why? A book gives permanence to the spoken and easily forgotten word. Only because God's commission was obediently carried out were the prophetic books, then in the form of parchment scrolls, still there and available to be picked up again in the days of Jesus: "Then the book of the prophet Isaiah was handed to Him" (Lk. 4:17).

Scripture, too, was the fundament of the new preaching of Jesus. What He had learned from it became the solid basis of His assurance of God at the beginning of His work, in the hour of His temptation in the desert (Matt. 4). Even at the end of His bodily existence on earth we see Him act as an interpreter of Scripture, when He accompanied the disciples on the way to Emmaus (Lk. 24:27). The church was founded on Scripture, and in Paul we read, "Bring me the cloak which I left in Troas when you come, and also the books, especially the parchments!" (2 Tim. 4:13).

In correspondence to the great importance of this book stands the urgent task of reading and studying it. Joshua is already being told, "Do not let the book of this law depart from your lips!" (Jos. 1:8). And Jesus presupposes that His audience, reading the Scriptures, accepts them as authority when He asks, "What is written? How do you read it?" (Matt. 12:3; Lk. 10:26). He accuses the Pharisees of "knowing neither Scripture nor the power of God" (Matt. 22:29). Therefore, in keeping with an Old Testament admonition (Is. 34:16), He challenges one and all to "Search the Scriptures, for you think you

SOME HISTORICAL DATA 13

have eternal life in it; and it is the one that witnesses of me!" (John 5:39).

Things are in their right order when, as in Berea during the Apostle Paul's second missionary journey, "They accepted the word willingly and searched daily in Scripture, whether these things were so" (Acts 17:11). Thus, the Christian faith becomes the "religion of the book." Oral proclamation, even the preaching of Jesus, must establish itself in accordance with Scripture.

God's Word is not only spoken, but written and printed. God's Word is not only intended to be heard, but also to be read. Of course, the reader of Scripture must not be satisfied with mere information, or with theoretical knowledge of what has been read. In the realm of the Christian faith, what counts is always acting on what one has learned. Eternal salvation depends on it. This is exactly what the last chapter of the

Bible has to say: "Behold, I am coming soon. Blessed is he who keeps the words of prophecy in this book" (Rev. 22:7).

Books—God's Tools in History

In 1963, the printing industry held an international exhibition in London, which was the product of a very intelligent idea. Using the original editions of about 400 books and pamphlets, the IPEX 63 demonstrated the effect which printing has had on the development of our whole civilization.

For this unique exhibition (running for ten days only) a detailed and richly illustrated catalog of all books on display was published.[1] In 1968 it appeared in German under the telling

---

1 J. Carter, P.H. Muir (eds.), *Printing and the Mind of Man. A Descriptive Catalogue Illustrating the Impact of Print on the Evolution of Western Civilization during Five Centuries*, (London: Cassell, 1967).

SOME HISTORICAL DATA 15

title "Books which changed the world." It reported on the contents and the mode of publication of these so eminently influential printings, beginning with the 1455 Gutenberg Bible of Mainz, all the way down to Einstein's "world formula" (published in 1925 in the minutes of a meeting of the Prussian Academy of the Sciences).

As one reads this book of more than 700 pages, one inevitably comes to the conclusion that *books make history*—much more so than the wars we always hear about in the history books. The selection of books in that exhibition naturally depended on the particular and subjective criteria used by the organizers, despite all honourable efforts to draw a universally valid picture. And it was of course also impossible to include the mass of large and small printed works which have had a part in shaping the progress of our intellectual and political history, some of which we might regard as of much greater significance than those titles which were included in the exhibition. But this was made clear beyond a shadow of doubt: books form history.

So what I would like to do now is to show by a few characteristic examples the decisive effects books have had in the history of Christianity. Especially it can be stated right from the start that books are closely linked to most Christian renewal movements. Almost always, renewal movements were initiated through books and/or they made intensive use of books as the medium of their dissemination and success. Let us begin with the Reformation!

The Reformation

Martin Luther at first assigned greater importance to *oral* preaching than to written or printed propagation. At one point during the actual years of reformation, he pointed out that

Christ neither gave His teaching in writing nor ordered it to be written down. Therefore, he said, it is "really not in the spirit of the New Testament to write books about Christian doctrine; rather, there should be good, scholarly, spiritually-minded and industrious preachers in all places, who would draw the living Word from the old Scriptures..."

Luther considered it "already a great corruption and ailment of the spirit" that people had felt the need to write books, and "if wishing would help, nothing better could be desired but that all books were put away across the board, and nothing would remain in the world, particularly among Christians, but only pure Scripture or the Bible." Nevertheless, it was indeed necessary to write, he says, in order to fight false teachers and heretics, so that wherever shepherds had turned out to be wolves, the sheep, or at least some of them, would be able to feed themselves.[2] Thus, books were to undercut false doctrines dominating the day, to reach out to individuals and preserve them in the true faith. Despite this rather reserved opinion about Christian literature, Luther himself wrote extensively. His biography actually almost consists of his bibliography, a list of his writings. Brochures and books mark the high points of his life.

What is a definite fact in all political revolutions, i.e., that they were preceded by a war of pamphlets, is also true of the spiritual revolution of the Protestant Reformation. Luther made extensive use of the medium of pamphlets or short tracts. In each of them, some urgent question of the day could be taken up and dealt

---

[2] From Luther's Church Postil (Sermon on the day of Epiphany), *Ausgewahlte Werke*, eds. H.H. Borcherdt, G. Merz, 3rd ed., suppl. vol. 4, (Munich, 1960), p. 298 (not in the American Edition of Luther's Works).

SOME HISTORICAL DATA

with. We are to think even of the 95 Theses less as a piece of parchment nailed to the door of the castle church at Wittenberg, but rather as going out in the form of one of the most widely and rapidly distributed pamphlets of the time. The numerous short tracts of the following years were of equal effect.[3]

---

3 "The vast quantities of pamphlets issued in Germany (630 have been listed from the years 1520 to 1530) leave no doubt that without the printing press the course of the German Reformation might have been different. Luther's own writings constitute a third of German books printed in the first four decades of the sixteenth century; his address *To the Christian Nobility of the German Nation* (August 1520) was reprinted thirteen times in two years; *Concerning Christian Liberty* (September 1520) came out eighteen times before 1526." J. Carter/P.H. Muir; p. XXXIX. Compare S.H. Steinberg, *Five hundred Years of Printing*, (London: Faber, 1959), p. 103: "Thirty editions of Luther's *Sermon on Indulgences* and 21 editions of his *Sermon on the Right Preparation of the Heart*—authorized and piratical—poured from the presses within two years (1518-20). Over 4,000 copies of his address *To the Christian Nobility* were sold within five days in 1520."

In addition to this came the striking success of the first edition of Luther's translation of the New Testament in 1521. The first printing of 3,000 copies was sold at one and a half guilders each, which was then equivalent to the weekly wages of a carpenter. Despite this high price, the first printing was sold out in three months, and it was followed by a large number of reprints, both legal and illegal.[4]

The Reformation was a change in the thought and life of nations through literature. Oral preaching would have been locally confined, while literature had unrestricted effectiveness. Luther even won some of his best fellow fighters, e.g., Melanchthon, through the fact that they first read his writings, then came into personal communication with him.

---

[4] After the first edition in September, the second edition of the New Testament was called for in December. "Fourteen authorized and 66 pirated editions came out within the next two years." S.H. Steinberg, p. 104.

SOME HISTORICAL DATA

The effectiveness of his writings caused Luther to change his mind about the significance of the book for Christian proclamation. He began to see preaching and writing side by side. Thus, in 1524, in the midst of the battle for the permanent establishment of the Reformation, he wrote,

> Take care now, promote and help promote the holy Gospel. Teach and defend, speak, write and promote, preach, how the laws of man are nothing. Let us drive this another two years and you will see where...the worms and storms will be; like smoke they will vanish. But if we do not teach this and do not bring such truth amongst the people, then it will remain, even if we would instigate a thousand rebellions against it. But you see what has been the result

of just this one year, that we have driven and written such truth? How short and how narrow has the cover become for the Papists.[5]

So there is a principle of action of which we must be taking heed again today, even where the battle front has changed!

For Luther, the fight by way of the printed word is a matter of principle. For, he said, change, reformation, and revival for the Christian can never be brought about by violence, but only through the Word, preached, written, and printed.

The Reformed church also took note of the effectiveness of the printed word. Calvin provided hard-pressed fellow believers in France with the weapons of theological literature.

---

5 M. Luther, *Ausgewahlte Werke* (see n. 2), 2nd ed., vol. 4, (Munich, 1938), p. 12f. (not in the American edition).

Wherever he or his messengers would not be free to travel, his writings made their impact instead. Secular history has shrewdly observed that John Knox achieved the breakthrough for the Reformation in his native Scotland through a "pamphleteering campaign" of six successive tracts.[6] Here again, one man, and from exile at that, reached the masses of a nation, bypassing the ruling class. The printed word turned out to be the lever with which the enemy was lifted from his saddle.

Pietism

A second example of the quite remarkable usage of literature as a medium of Christian renewal is the beginning of Pietism. The origins of Pietism date back neither to a famous sermon nor to a mass rally, but to the publication date of a piece of less than seventy

6 J. Carter/P.H. Muir, p. 49: ten polemical tracts.

pages, the *Pia Desideria* of Ph. J. Spener. It was a manifesto for church reform which was first published as the introduction to a larger work of another author, which Spener edited. Later appearing separately, this tract found extremely wide distribution. After that, everybody asked for Spener's printed sermons. Again: reform by way of small tracts!

We can study exemplary use of the printing press as the medium for propagating new convictions, which led to a revival of dried-up areas of Christendom, in the work of August Hermann Francke, Spener's younger friend and spiritual heir.

This eminent theologian and founder of the large orphanages of Halle already thought in his "Great Essay" of 1704, outlining his plans, of the creation of "many small tracts, which should be distributed to the people in great numbers. They are not very costly, can be read quickly and easily be passed to another person. For the building of the Kingdom of God, they make a greater contribution than bulky tomes."[7] As a proof, Francke pointed to the successful Christian literature work in late 17th century Britain.

In one of the biographies of Francke, E. Beyreuther has given special attention to the publishing activity of this theologian. He reports that soon after founding the pharmacy of the orphanage, whose profits supported his charitable enterprises, Francke established his own publishing house, which at first served the distribution of his sermons.

Here again, a task taken up with faith and courage also finds the right people for cooperation. A thirty-year-old man was among the audience of Francke's first sermon; it moved

---

7 E. Beyreuther, *August Hermann Franke*, (Marburg, 1956), p. 214. 8.

him so deeply that at that hour he devoted his life to God's work on earth. Heinrich J. Ehlers opened his Christian bookstore in the former ballroom which had served as a lecture hall for Francke.

Soon, Ehlers added a printer's shop. Next, he opened branch stores at Leipzig, Berlin, and Frankfurt/Mainz. He not only excelled through extraordinary professional competence, which won him the respect of his colleagues, but quietly worked among them and beyond as a competent Christian counsellor. His booth at the Leipzig Book Fair became a spiritual power centre.[8]

Apart from the distribution of small tracts (in one year, 1717, Francke's publishing house turned out about 80,000 copies), there was the founding of the first Bible Society in evangelical Christendom, in 1710, under the name of

8 Ibid., p. 170f.

Francke's friend, Count von Canstein. Its first Bible was printed in 1712, and until von Canstein's death in 1719, twenty-eight printings of the New Testament (100,000 copies) and sixteen printings of the whole Bible (80,000 copies) were published. It was this Bible Society which for the first time in the industry worked with standing type (composition). Thus a greater initial investment in the long run led to much lower prices for the Bibles produced.[9]

In addition to small tracts and the distribution of Bibles, Francke worked on the publication of theological literature, which was to serve the urgently-needed education of preachers. Already as early as 1717, he produced 12,000 copies of theological titles. They added to the wide influence of printed sermons and pamphlets the dimension of depth.

9 Ibid., p. 211f.

Francke further took an interest in the development and publication of educational literature, especially of schoolbooks. Finally, we must not forget that on the basis of his wide international correspondence Francke was able to found one of the first regularly-published German newspapers. This simultaneously opened up the valuable opportunity for a Christian interpretation of world affairs.

In summing up, it was the intention of Francke and his friends universally to use the printing press as a medium of Christian proclamation. Their wide-range success confirmed the original depth of vision.

Methodism

Exactly the same results may be found in early Methodism, the renewal movement associated with John Wesley. I would like to select just a few small points from which we may still learn today.

SOME HISTORICAL DATA

For Wesley, following Christ meant at a certain point in his life that he must be willing to preach open-air sermons. He began to preach in the streets because there were no churches for a large section of the poorer populace. Having become uncertain of the venture because of the attacks of outsiders and the hesitance of some of his friends, Wesley cast lots on whether to continue. He received the answer: "Preach and print!"[10] In an exceptional manner, Wesley stood by this precept until his dying day.

It has been said that he did not let one single week of his life go by without having prepared something for the printer, either a chapter of a book or a pamphlet, printed sermon, or tract. Like Francke, he emphasized, "We must give special importance to supplying the poor with shorter, cheaper and simpler books than those

---

10 J. Schempp. *Seelsorge und Seelenfuhrung bei J. Wesley*, (Stuttgart, 1949), p. 143 n. 336.

that have existed up to now," and began to write many small tracts himself. Later, larger books were added. Often written in the style of real or fictitious dialogues, they were tools of pastoral ministry, admonition and defense.[11]

Secondly, Wesley used the medium of the book to further the education of his preachers. Since he was unable to establish an actual school for them, he created the so-called "Christian Library"—a standard collection of fifty books partly from his own pen, partly consisting of extracts from the most important books of Christian tradition. It was a kind of correspondence course for the present and future generations of Methodist preachers.

But he did not only desire to better educate his preachers, he also saw in them above all those who were to bring Christian literature

---

11 J. Telford, *The Life of John Wesley*, (London: Hodder, 1886), p. 330.

to the people. If the 19th century coined the phrase, "Every Christian a missionary through books!", Wesley emphasized, "Every preacher a distributor of Christian literature."

The Methodist preachers covered the circuit of congregations assigned to them on horseback, and all they carried with them were two saddle bags; one contained a change of clothes, the other held a supply of Methodist books for sale.

Wesley had great confidence in the power of the book, and he expected his fellow workers to promote the sale of books with all possible means. I quote: "Sometimes I am amazed that not all the preachers among us are convinced that the distribution of our tracts to all congregations is invaluable. Take a certain title with you when you first make the round through the congregations. The next time take another book. Preach at every place, and invite the congregation after the sermon to buy the relevant tract and to read it."[12]

To another preacher he wrote about a recently published book, "Dear friend! Promote the sale of this book publicly as well as in private conversation. Do not spare an effort to strain yourself and thus prove your love of the Truth for mankind, and of your loving friend and brother John Wesley."[13]

It is important not just to sell or buy books, but also to read them. Wesley not only promoted the production of Christian literature, he was first of all an enormous reader. It has been said that he was the man who had seen more of England than anyone else. When travelling on horseback, he would read. He read theology, history, poetry, he read philosophical and scientific literature.

---

12 Ibid., p. 211.
13 Garth Lean, *John Wesley, Anglican*, (London: Blandford Press, 1964), p. 64.

For he wished to learn from everybody, and learn to the last day of his life.[14] Much of his reading would then be applied in his preaching.

Wesley always rode without the reins, in order to be able to read; and on his 60,000 miles of travels, he almost never fell. Later, when friends put a carriage at his disposal, he first of all had a bookshelf built into it. There he read for hours in greatest solitude. He was not so different from us: he had to fight for the quiet hours of reading.

To his fellow fighters he wrote: "How does it come that the state of our congregations is not better? There are many reasons for this. But the main reason is this, that we ourselves do not have more understanding. And why is it that we don't have more understanding? Answer: because we are lazy. We are forgetful of the first of our rules: be industrious, do not go idle for

14 J. Telfordr, p.266 and 362.

one moment! Faithlessness in using our time also results in a lack of sanctity."[15]

This was a primary rule for the Methodist preachers: from four to five o'clock in the morning they would read the Scriptures together with the exegetical notes published by Wesley, and the hours from six to noon were spent over several parts of the "Christian Library" or similar literature. This portion of the Wesleyan preacher's daily schedule often gave ground to posterity for terror and admiration, and may perhaps be too difficult to follow today. However, it can provoke us to reconsider where we put the emphases of our own life's work.

The Clapham Sect: Christian Literature in the Fight for Social Reform

For someone looking into the history of books as tools of God's salvation in the story of mankind,

15 J. Schempp, p. 229 and n. 551.

one of the most glorious examples is the battle waged by the "Clapham Sect," the great William Wilberforce and his friends, for the abolition of the slave trade and for "the Reformation of Manners" in England. There can hardly be a more instructive case of Christians taking upon themselves the responsibility to change the course of their nation, or a more brilliant illustration of the teamwork of people with their variety of gifts, and hardly a better example of the all-around Christian use of the printing press. We can look only at this facet of that whole magnificent story.[16]

In the beginning, there was just a handful of evangelical Christians determined to reverse the destructive trends in the society of their land. Of them, a significant number had found their faith and their purpose in life through reading a book. John Newton was the captain of a

16 Garth Lean, *God's Politician. William Wilberforce's Struggle*, (London: Darton, Longman and Todd, 1980), p. 30.

slave ship, when in the middle of the Atlantic he read Thomas a Kempis' *The Imitation of Christ*. It changed his life. William Wilberforce, after participating fully in his youth in the entertainments of the wealthy ruling class and its enlightened thoughtlessness concerning God, was finally awakened by reading a book, Philip Doddridge's *The Rise and Progress of Religion in the Soul*. For a decisive interview, he went to John Newton, who had become a pastor in London.

John Newton's own book *Cardiphonia* aroused the interest of Hannah More, by then already a successful and fashionable writer. She felt it was full of "vital experimental religion," showing the reality of God, and the difference between religion as *an* essential and *the* essential of life.[17]

Again, a book, written by Wilberforce in 1797, and the manifesto of his commencing

---

17 M.G. Jones, *Hannah More*, (Cambridge: University Press, 1952), pp. 87 and 89.

battle—*A Practical View of the Prevailing Religious System of Professed Christians in the Higher and Middle Classes in This Country, Contrasted with Real Christianity*—was the clarion call for, among many, Legh Richmond, who became both a popular preacher and prodigious tract writer. So, both the people and the actual campaigns were first sparked by books.

James Ramsey, who had been a pastor in the West Indies for twenty-seven years and knew the evils of the slave trade through firsthand knowledge, published his "Essay on the Treatment of Slaves" in 1782. Six years later, William Wilberforce was ready to take up the matter in Parliament. In a concentrated effort, Hannah More simultaneously published the poem "The Slave Trade" to help arouse public opinion.

Later, when Wilberforce's attempts at abolition, although constantly repeated, were to prove in vain for many years, Hannah More's

Cheap Repository Tracts kept the slavery issue before tens of thousands of readers through a period of "hope deferred."[18] When Richard Cobden planned his strategy for the abolition of the Corn Laws in 1840, he consciously modelled it on the evangelical antislavery movement.[19] Authorities speak of it as one of the earliest propaganda campaigns for social reform in English history.

The *Cheap Repository Tracts* were Hannah More's weapon to counter the atheist, amoral, and subversive ideas coming over from France in the day of the Revolution. She and her fellow workers studied the cheap popular chapbooks and broadsheets closely and had their own stories, ballads, and comments printed on the same coarse brown paper and with

---

18 Ibid., p. 91.
19 I. Bradley, *The Call to Seriousness. The Evangelical Impact on the Victorians*, (London: Jonathan Cape, 1976), p. 174.

similarly colourful titles and lively woodcuts. By means of subscriptions from well-to-do friends, the series—three numbers came out in a month—could be sold cheaper than its worldly counterparts.

Christians who were able to do so bought the tracts in bulk and helped to distribute them wherever they could. After one and a half months, 300,000 copies were sold, and after a year, two million. The *Cheap Repository Tracts* became "a principal part of the English cottager's library,"[20] forming the substance of popular reading in Ireland, and in 1821 the whole series was reprinted for Scotland. This enterprise lasted only three or four years, but then the Religious Tract Society took over, which published at a rate of ten million copies of fifty titles each year through the next fifty years. It has been said without exaggeration that Hannah More

20 M.G. Jones, p. 83.

and her friends "helped raise the standards of living, of technology…of ethics, of generations then unborn."[21]

With a series of extremely successful books, Hannah More tried to reach the ruling classes and make them aware of the responsibility they had for their moral demeanour in the limelight of society.

Of course, the opponents of the Clapham persuasion also had been using the press intelligently and successfully. So much did Hannah More think in terms of strategy that she even wrote a novel, *Coelebs in Search of a Wife*, in order to invade the popular circulating libraries of her time, and she did so with eleven printings in nine months and 30,000 copies sold in America up to 1833 when she died.

---

21 Mary Alden Hopkins, *Hannah More and Her Circle*, (New York: Longmans, 1947), p. 220. See also G.H. Spinney, *The Cheap Repository Tracts: Transactions of the Bibliographical Society*, (London: 1940), and S.G. Green, *The Story of the Religious Tract Society*, 1899.

In 1842, Charles Mudie, another evangelical, founded a circulating library run according to the standards of his faith; within twenty years it had become England's biggest, with 25,000 subscribers.[22] W.H. Smith, a staunch Methodist and the owner of railway station bookshops, helped towards the same aim through a careful selection of titles.

Other means of influencing the nation through print were the *Christian Observer*, the monthly magazine edited by the Clapham group, as well as a book of family prayers which saw thirty-one printings in two years, and an evangelical hymn book with a sale of 150,000 copies in a few months in 1833.[23] Later on, special emphasis was laid on the publication of cheap and popular biographies, especially missionary biographies, which would help people to a purpose in life.

22 I. Bradley. p. 98.
23 Ibid., p. 65.

There is no space here to describe the phenomenal expansion of the Bible Society founded in 1804, which is a whole story in itself.

Historians have always expressed surprise at the remarkable change of the moral and religious climate in England between the eighteenth and nineteenth centuries. Suddenly the atheism, loose living, and cruelty of the eighteenth century were no longer fashionable, and the ruling class had begun to think in terms of social reform: abolition of slavery, reform of the penal code and of prisons, and the host of factory legislation. One is reminded of the remark of one well-meaning but skeptical bishop who in the seventeen nineties welcomed the books written by Hannah More with the cautious words, "if any writing can do much good in a country debauched by its riches and prosperity."[24] Well, it did, singularly so. Once

24 M.G. Jones, p. 112.

more, books and pamphlets proved effective tools in the hands of Christians who were willing to take up God's commission to sustain His creation and to help heal the hurts of a humanity always tending to deteriorate through the effects of evil.

The Use of Literature in the Beginning of Foreign Missions

It is befitting to add to this series of instances of the use of literature in the renewal of Christendom, its use in foreign missions, which is in more than one sense also a renewal movement of Christianity. The Moravian Brethren, pioneers of the evangelical movement of missions, say about themselves, "Towards the heathen we use all kinds of methods of bringing them the gospel of Christ. We abundantly share with them the printed booklets which they read among themselves and send from one place to the other."[25]

Already the extensive mission of the Jesuits in Asia in the sixteenth century had made use of the printer's press everywhere. In China, the Jesuits wrote books which, judged from their content, can be subsumed under the category of pre-evangelism; these books found wide distribution and actually became a part of the history of Chinese literature. In fact, in Korea this literature led to the conversion of scholars to Christianity, before they had ever seen a missionary.[26]

Similarly, we hear from an Indian bishop who found the way to the Christian faith as a Muslim, far away from any mission station, by

---

25 As quoted in: A. Lehmann, "Unbekannte Pioniere der Christlichen Literatur", in *Christ und Buch. Oekumenische Erfahrungen der Kirchen mit dem Buch in aller Welt*, ed. O. Schnetter, (Wuppertal/ Stuttgart, 1972), p. 91.

26 N. Moritzen, ibid., p. 91.

SOME HISTORICAL DATA

reading a gospel.[27] In India, the Francis Xavier mission very early turned to the printing of Christian books. Already in 1578, the first little book appeared in the Tamil language.

In 1706, the first evangelical missionaries landed in Southern India; two years later, they had a printing press sent from their home base. Upon specification by the missionaries, Tamil letters were produced at Halle in Germany and sent out to Tranquebar. Soon afterwards, a casting furnace and a paper mill were put into service on the spot. One of the press's first two printings was Luther's *Small Catechism*.[28]

When William Carey, the "saintly cobbler" and Baptist missionary, came to India in 1793, he is said to have looked for a second-hand printing press during the first days of his stay in order to be able to print tracts and the

27 Ibid., p. 101.
28 Ibid., p. 96.

Bible.[29] Wherever he and his colleagues went to preach, they also distributed books and pamphlets. Later, in Serampore, he worked for the translation, printing, and distribution of the Bible on a remarkable scale. Famous is the picture of that work given in a letter by W. Ward, Carey's fellow-worker and printer:

> As you enter, you see your cousin in a small room, dressed in a white jacket, reading or writing, and looking over the office, which is more than 170 feet long. There you find Indians translating the Scriptures into the different tongues, or correcting proof sheets. You observe, laid out in cases, types in Arabic, Persian, Nagari, Telegu, Punjabi, Bengali, Marathi, Chinese, Oriya,

---

29 A.H. Oussoren, *William Carey, especially his Missionary Principles*, (Leiden: Sijthoff, 1945), p. 210.

Burmese, Kanarese, Greek, Hebrew, and English. Hindus, Mussulmans, and Christian Indians are busy composing, correcting, distributing. Next are four men throwing off the Scripture sheets in the different languages, others folding the sheets and delivering them to the large storeroom, and six Mussulmans do the binding. Beyond the office are the varied type-casters, besides a group of men making ink, and in a spacious open walled-round place, our paper-mill, for we manufacture our own paper.[30]

Carey himself experienced how God's word in print would reach out beyond the borders of established missionary activity:

30 As quoted in J.H. Morrison, *William Carey, Cobbler and Pioneer*, (London: Hodder, n.d.), p. 120f.

Seventeen years after, when the Mission extended to the old capital of Dacca, there were found several villages of Hinduborn peasants who had given up idol worship, were renowned for their truthfulness, and as searching for a true teacher come from God, called themselves "Satyagurus." They traced their new faith to a much-worn book kept in a wooden box in one of their villages. No one could say whence it had come; all they knew was that they had possessed it for many years. It was Carey's first Bengali version of the New Testament of our Lord and Saviour Jesus Christ.[31]

It is self-evident that printers must have readers. Thus, educational work always goes

---

31 Ibid., p. 123.

parallel to the preaching of the gospel. Even today, eighty percent of all schools, e.g. in Africa, are mission schools. In India, it was the Christian mission which carried the written language to the mass of the people. William Carey created the first Indian newspaper in that language. Apart from this, it was of course the tract literature which found a vast field of dissemination in a people poor but hungry for education and salvation.

Some have thrown up the alternative: Which is more important, preaching or the propagation of Christian literature? Arno Lehmann, a theologian of missions from East Germany, answers this false alternative with the classic statement: "The history of missions is full of priorities." He points out that medical and educational work are more and more being taken up by national governments. "But," he concludes, "the way of literature remains open. Very soon it may be the only way in which the older churches can help the younger ones."[32]

With that, our attention is finally directed to the fact that literature is not only able to serve the unlimited spreading of the Gospel, but also the deepening and consolidation of its understanding: especially in those places where circumstances temporarily prevent public preaching. Thus, it is a remarkable fact that the work of the Gospel among the Gallas in Ethiopia, for example, survived a critical number of years when threatened with extinction because of the expulsion of missionaries in World War I, because, among other things, Christian literature in the vernacular had been created and distributed from the very beginning. The Bible and other Christian books remained a reminder of the oral preaching, and served as the standard which prevented an alteration and corruption of the message received.

---

32 Ibid., p. 106.

SOME HISTORICAL DATA 51

Excursion: The Role of Literature in the Political Revolutions of Modern History

We will conclude this survey of the relevance of literature with a section on the use of books in the more recent secular history. It can serve as material for comparison and also teach thoughtful Christians one or two things.

We have seen with what deliberate awareness and insight Christians in the past have made use of literature as an important tool, and may well ask ourselves whether we have not been far too indifferent compared with their circumspection and eagerness. It might also be useful to study those forces of the secular world which have actually appropriated much from the practices of our Christian forefathers. Perhaps we will allow ourselves to be stimulated by such a comparison, pick up the heritage of the fathers, and begin to work again on the task of Christian literary mission much more energetically.

As mentioned in the beginning, history shows that all revolutions of the modern age were initiated by a campaign of printed materials of various kinds. A war of ideas precedes the physical battles and directs these. This is true already of the 17th century English revolution, in which individual pamphlets, such as those of John Lilburne, proved their capacity of awakening the masses of the people to political consciousness and political action. What we earlier observed with Luther and John Knox is here repeated on a secular level.

In the decades preceding the French Revolution of 1789, the traditional ruling classes were discredited and intellectually disarmed through a flood of pamphlets which propagated the new ideas. When the sentiment reached its boiling point and the first offensive encroachments took place, the ancient regime had already lost its credibility and justification in the eyes of the public. It had nothing with which to counter the attack on the ideological level. Since that time, attentive observers have come to recognize the power of ideas. Today, therefore, in an age when (at least theoretically) all social strata participate in public life, every step of the government (or of any given social group) must be accompanied by its public justification. The age of propaganda has begun.

Regarding the various forms of literary warfare of those decades, it is worth noting the seemingly curious fact that apart from the pamphlet literature, it was the famous seventeen-volume *Encyclopedia* of Diderot and his friends (published 1751-1765), which shaped the thinking of the age and intellectually outmaneuvered the powers that be. All the great encyclopedias of the 19th and 20th centuries propagate certain world views. In Germany, we see at the same time how journals are turned into tactical weapons, thus e.g. Gottsched's *Amusements of the Mind and Wit* (1741-1749) and Lessing's *Hamburg Dramaturgy* (1768-1769) which did not restrict themselves to recording events in the form of annals, but with varying contributions pursued one single (in this case literary) objective.[33]

At the present time, regarding the use of the medium of literature, one can probably learn most from the Communists. V.I. Lenin reportedly once stated, "I would rather write a pamphlet than speak at 20 mass rallies." It is generally known that a crowd can be aroused on the spot. But a public speech will rarely effect a lasting change in a person. One picks up a few fleeting bits of information and impressions. But where people sit at home and continuously listen to the author, their thinking is shaped

---

33 S.H. Steinberg, *Die Schwarze Kunst. 500 Jahre Buchwesen*, (Munich, 1961), pp. 292f. (Only in the German version of the book mentioned in n. 3).

SOME HISTORICAL DATA

much more deeply. Certainly we cannot bring anyone to rebirth through a book; that can only be brought about by the Holy Spirit. But we can point out the way to every reader and raise an irrefutable challenge.

Incidentally, Lenin remained true to his preference. In the lean years after the abortive revolution of 1905, he sustained and directed the Communist Movement in Czarist Russia from his Swiss exile—not much different from John Knox!—showing the way in questions of immediate interest through newspaper articles and pamphlets. Similar to France, in Russia the revolution of 1917 was spearheaded through print and paper. The Communists were using all forms of literature to promote revolutionary consciousness.[34] When ideas have taken hold of

---

[34] Quite illuminating in this respect is the propaganda work of Communist Willi Munzenberg in the nineteen twenties and thirties. See B. Gross, *Willi Munzenberg. Eine politische Biographie*, (Stuttgart, 1967).

the hearts of people, then those people take up arms and carry out the revolutions about which we read in the history books, which often only tell us about the political and military results of an intellectual movement.

Karl Marx reduced this fact to the terse formula: "An idea becomes a material force when it takes hold of the masses." For the relationship between the original idea of the individual and its realization by the many, the pamphlet and the book serve as the medium or the driving belt without which the idea remains powerless.

Consequently, the Communists still today have a very clear knowledge of what a book can do. Therefore, as one travels through the Iron Curtain, e.g. at the checkpoint Berlin-Friedrichstrasse, much more important than the customary, "Any alcoholic beverages?" will be the question, "Are you carrying printed materials?" This question is never omitted.

As I was travelling to East Berlin some time ago, I had two brochures of theological content with me, small items of forty pages each. Nevertheless, the customs officer sent me back: I had to obtain a locker on the Western side and deposit my two booklets there until I returned at night.

The Communists are very well aware of the power which the printed word has had in their own revolution, and now they do not want to incur the same thing at the hands of other people. From this aspect we can also understand how disturbed the Soviet authorities were about the pen of that one individual, Solzhenitsyn. One man all of a sudden becomes a world force—through his books. Had he said all the things that he wrote, in the classroom or in the streets of the town where he was living as a mathematics teacher, the world would have heard nothing of it. But the fact that he wrote and that it was duplicated, printed, and spread proves that, compared with the spoken word, the written word is—as it were—like dynamite.

For Marxism, the concept holds true: The mass media, amongst them book and newspaper, are the carriers of the ideological battle. Therefore, in the area of its influence, the Communist party always claims, if not monopoly, then at least complete control over all literary production. That obviously is the conclusion they draw from the knowledge about the power of the printed word.

A study about the increasing muzzling of Christian literary work under the Nazi government can also give important insights. The Nazis brought the book trade under their control and decided that Christian literature could only be sold in special Christian bookstores. In addition, only those who were allowed to write or work as publishers were registered in the so-called Reichsschrifttumskammer (Chamber of

Literature). The printing of texts from other sources became a criminal offence.

This was finally applied to all Christian organizations, with the exception of the church authorities submissive to National Socialism, so that according to the letter of the relevant decree, church congregations and Christian associations were not even allowed to mimeograph texts on their own equipment. A further possibility arose—and under similar conditions is present still today—through state management and allotment of the paper needed for printing. The significance of this can be seen in the fact that for the Wurttemberg Bible Society, by far the largest German Bible publisher (producing more than four million Bibles between 1932 and 1937), from mid-1941 on "not one kilogramme of paper for the printing of Bibles on demand inside Germany was approved."[35]

35 H. Brunotte, in: *Christ und Buch*, (see n. 25), p. 180.

We know to what extent the battle over the right to and possibilities of printing Bibles and other Christian literature is still continuing to this day in many countries of the world. In his contribution about "The Spiritual Function of Christian Literature in the Emergency of the Church," Fr. Bartsch has described the first twenty years of the Evangelical Publishing House in East Berlin under Communist rule, with its restrictions and its ups and downs.[36] Indeed, Marxism in particular assigns great value to printed materials for the ideological struggle which necessarily precedes every political upheaval. This is shown by the fact that wherever a Communist party is forced into illegality, one of their first priorities is always the establishment of secret printer's shops and the procurement of the necessary paper.

Whether they are underground or in power and trying to control the underground, for the

36 Ibid., p. 208f.

Communists every last piece of mimeographing equipment and every box of xerox paper is of special interest. It is the Christians in the Soviet Union itself who are now apparently learning again from the Communists.

As we sum up our overview of history and the Christian use of literature in it, we will agree with what Milton once had to say: "Books are not absolutely dead...I know they are as lively, and as vigourously productive, as those fabulous Dragon's teeth; and being sown up and down, may chance to spring up armed men."[37]

---

37 As quoted in *AB, Bookman's Weekly*, (Clifton, New York), June 16, 1980, title page.

Present-Day Opportunities

The Future of Books

In General

Over the past two decades, some culture critics have been eager to proclaim "the end of the Gutenberg era" and the dawning of the age of television. Only a few years ago you could hear people predict that by 1985 at the latest books would be the old-fashioned remainder of a past epoch and not found in many families at all. We had polls taken which seemed to say that books quickly became an "also-ran" in the race with television.

In the meantime, voices pronouncing doom on books have become less noisy. In the mid-seventies, some countries, after a passing phase of recession, witnessed a comfortable amount of growth of the book trade, with figures sometimes beyond the average growth of the retail trade. If the demographic polls seemed to indicate that more books are being bought than read, the figures of borrowing in public libraries, which have shown a steady increase, pointed to the opposite.[38] The end of reading is not yet in sight.[39]

---

38 In the Federal Republic of Germany, the increase in recent years was between 10 and 20 percent, according to D.E. Zimmer, Die Zeit weekly, Dec. 26, 1975.

39 In his interesting study *Book Publishing, Book Selling, and Book Reading: A Report to the Book Marketing Council of the Publishers Association* (London, April 1979), Peter H. Mann notes (p. 5f) that in Britain roughly one third of the population reads regularly, one third almost never read—whereas it would be possible and necessary to help the last third towards more familiarity with books. A fact worth

PRESENT-DAY OPPORTUNITIES 65

A highly technicized society could not afford a "secondary illiteracy." The paperback market especially has not yet exhausted its possibilities. In some countries, publishers have only recently begun to reprint whole sets of classical authors in paperback form—not without success.

I am particularly impressed by the observation over the last few years that many topics of general interest have been published first as books, then through television. Not least in the United States, shrewd authors who plan the selling of their wares strategically have chosen the book, not the newspaper or television, as their primary medium, even in cases of reports with only temporary appeal. As soon as the

---

probing into is that reading for enjoyment declines steeply with children 10 to 14 years old (ibid., p. 7)! In the United States, the Book Industry Study expects books buyers to spend 11.2 billion dollars on books in 1983, up from 7.2 billion in 1979, with a real increase of 14 percent in numbers of books published.

publication date of such a book approaches, in cases of general interest, television and newspapers will report about it anyway, or else there is the possibility of the publisher's paying for a spot on commercial television or radio. The debates of the last years have shown the advantages of the printed book over the mass media.

Even a prominent expert in communication electronics, Karl Steinbuch of the Technical University of Karlsruhe, West Germany, speaks out for the book. He reminds us that the book does not require technical preparations. One does not need an infrastructure of energy supply or special playback equipment. A book is independent of broadcasting hours and is always available. It even allows for individually adapted speed of usage. You can pause when you feel a break is needed, then continue. The television presentation often rushes by the viewer, whereas the effect of reading a book is more lasting.[40] Others observe that moving pictures quickly tend to arouse emotions which can be just as quickly forgotten afterwards. The book invites its readers to cool consideration and quiet decision.

We all experience constantly that a book is the handiest medium. Reading on a train or plane does not inconvenience your fellow travelers in any way. Using one's pencil one may even enter a silent conversation with the author. In most cases the book is easier to handle than the respective tape recorder. There is no substitute for the book. In view of these factors, one almost comes to the conclusion that at worst the book can only remove itself from the public mind through a prohibitive increase in price. Of course, everybody is aware of price hikes in the paper industry which are without precedent. At the same time also, the cost of printing has

40 German daily *Die Welt* (Hamburg), Oct. 10, 1974.

gone up considerably. Employees in the printing industry have always taken a pride in leading the field regarding wages, and they are on the alert today, too. Of course, this is a must in times of an inflationary economy. However, that whole situation should lead publishers to renewed efforts in order at least to slow down the rise of book prices through inventiveness, rationalization, and cooperation.

We are all familiar with the argument of the apple-growing farmer who said to his wife, "Thank God, we'll have a smaller harvest this year." That means prices are up, income will be substantially the same, but we'll have less trouble. Could there be a similar attitude in the book industry? I have heard some people defend even a major price increase for books, saying the reader will just have to learn the cultural value of books. In recent years, the increase in the price of books had indeed exceeded that of food, etc., but then that was thought to be quite appropriate.

To me this self-confident and complacent attitude seems rather dangerous. It seems to admit that books should become articles of luxury, accessible to the rich (as in former centuries); it even sounds like saying if there are no more books at all in the future, it is the fault of the reader: he was not willing to pay what we felt we could charge. I hope that the future of the book trade will lie in the opposite direction, and that, should lean years indeed now follow the fat ones, they will see the book people exercising themselves in every imaginable way in order to help books reach their readers.

The Future of Christian Books
What I have said just before should be even more valid for Christian publishers and

booksellers. I am convinced that the Christian book trade today finds itself in a particularly promising and provocative situation, much more so and for different reasons than the general book trade.

Some years ago, an opinion poll taken in West Germany substantiated what we all knew to be true in the countries of Western Europe and the Nordic North. This particular poll showed that eighty-five percent of the present membership of the national church did not consider leaving the church. However, only twelve percent said that they had some kind of a concrete relationship to the life of the church. That situation cries for a medium which will go out to the large number of people instead of waiting for them to come to the church. There are therefore vast opportunities for evangelism and pre-evangelism through literature.

Also, we know that in recent years the church has been the object of much criticism, whereas the Christian faith has found a new interest. Here again the Christian book is the natural conversation partner for those who are fascinated by Christianity, if not by the church.

A similar situation seems to exist in Japan, where according to statistics made available through the World Council of Churches three times as many people are interested in Christianity as actually are members of a church; Christian writers are widely read and discussed.[41]

All this calls for intelligent exploration. One of the leading figures of the German book trade has expressed his conviction that the range of influence of the religious books could possibly be doubled. He especially pointed to religious brochures, biographies of Christian

41 *From Mexico City to Bangkok*, Geneva (WCC), 1972, p. 4.

personalities, Christian novels, stories from the mission fields, and books on current problems seen from a Christian perspective as proven and successful tools of Christian propagation.[42]

I don't think it is exaggerating to say that evangelical publishers especially have already recognized and seized their opportunities and that the expansion of Christian publishing during the past decade can be substantiated from their annual balance sheets. I believe this is true for a number of countries, in Europe as well as in North America.

---

42 *Christ und Buch* (see n. 25), pp. 269 and 273. The story of the distribution of the Bible would require a chapter in itself. Recent polls in West Germany signal that four million Protestant Christians read the Bible frequently or regularly (in 1967, the respective figure was 1.5 million). The Wurttemberg Bible Society produced 2.09 million Bibles or parts thereof in 1979, as compared to 1.47 in 1978. In December 1980, the Society opened the world's largest Bible printing works, where 170 employees look after one million different editions of the Bible, published in fifty languages.

Wherever the Christian book trade favoured the authors of the latest theological fashion, e.g., the God-is-Dead theology, they have come to feel the pinch. That boom was imaginary. The books of the God-is-Dead theology did not last. Those who hoped to make good business with the end of religion—logically also the end of business from religion—have been disappointed.

Others rightly quarrel with the uninviting language of the theologians in power, which hurts the trade. Indeed, it has been observed that some of the books dealing with hermeneutics are the least understandable. However, the biggest problem of the Christian book trade really has been that some publishers and booksellers have run along with the general relativism of values and standards in today's society. They lost their original sense of mission and were content merely to pass on information, and this in most cases consisted of nothing but the intellectual follies of the day.

A lack of conviction convinces no one. The emerging victors will therefore more and more be those, both in publishing and bookselling, who work from a missionary commitment and who—should it come to this—prefer a person of convictions willing to learn and professionally qualify, to an expert who has no spiritual perspective.

Ways and Means of Christian Work with Books

We have seen from the example of the Reformation how oral preaching and printed Gospel complemented and supported each other. Of course, Lenin, the Communist revolutionary, also did not exclude mass rallies when he stated his preference for the strategy with print. An American missionary has told the story of how in the years after World War II in a country in Asia he held an open-air Gospel meeting, and afterwards was approached by a man unknown to him who said: "You are incredibly foolish!" When the missionary asked for his reasons for such an extraordinary statement, the Asian answered: "Here you have thousands listening to you. Instead of furnishing them with tracts and books which could help deepen what they heard, you let them go away with some fleeting impression. You Christians are unbelievable dilettantes! We, however, will fill this country with our ideas from one end to the other, and we will do it by way of literature." A book continues working when the meeting has ended. It accompanies the audience back to their homes. It goes on speaking to them. Literature is the second leg of Christian proclamation.

If it is true that "every Christian is a missionary," then what our forefathers said a century ago must also be true: "Every Christian a distributor of Christian literature."

We are under the impression that at present and at least in the West the practical problems of Christian literary work are found not so much in production, but in distribution. Admittedly, there is also a paucity of good manuscripts in a number of fields; for example, in biblically committed theology, but also in Christian literature, novels, stories, especially for young people age fourteen and up. That is the other problem of the Christian publisher—but distribution seems to be the greatest bottleneck we are facing.

George Verwer, the founder of Operation Mobilization, who probably has more experience in this field than most other Christians, comes to the same result. (His book, by the way, is a must for all Christians who approach the work of missions through literature in any capacity.)[43]

---

43 George Verwer, *Revolution Through Reality in Christ*.

With the problem of distribution in mind we will now look at some of the more recent and unorthodox ways of Christian literature work. As I do not intend to trespass into the fields of the experts, I shall concentrate on forms of propagation of Christian literature below the level of publishing houses and bookshops.

The Individual as Representative of Christian Literature
The Book Depot

The simplest version of working with books consists of the individual Christian establishing at home a small stock of those books which have been useful or meaningful to him in the past months or years. He can give them away as a gift or—even better—sell them in the large circle of people he knows. It seems to be natural to feature one particular title for a given period of time. The following four rules have been set up to help sell a book in this way:

> I must have read the book myself.
> I should be seen with the book.
> I should talk to people about the book.
> I must have sufficient stock of the book for sale.

For more than 150 years, one Christian organization on the continent sent out young journeymen trained in the Bible to different towns. In their instructions we find something of an alertness for strategy which many of us can learn from:

> As he [the young journeyman] gets acquainted with the people in the place, he asks, of course with importunity, what religious books they read,

> whether they have a Bible or not, and, if there is a hunger for it, promises to provide them with Bibles and good and edifying literature for a modest price... He seeks to work through lending out his books, and, only should the other person urgently desire such a book, to sell it to them or give it as a gift...He then orders Bibles and religious literature from a central agency, distributes them, keeps account of the distribution and retains a list of the names of all those who received Bibles and with whom the purposes of mission seem to be effective...[44]

Thus young tradesmen were to be active as lay missionaries and as distributors of Christian

---

44 E. Staehelin, *Die Christentumsgesellschaft von der Zeit der Erweckung bis zur Gegenwart*, (Basel, 1974), p. 452f.

literature. It is quite possible that such a plan, consciously pursued, can grow beyond all expectations. Where it is known that someone is committed to the expansion of Christian literature work, he or she will often find larger opportunities.

One can participate in all kinds of Christian meetings and present one's books where such a service has not yet been established. We know of a quite recent experience where a mother and housewife in South Africa imported and sold Christian literature worth 4,000 pounds sterling in one year alone. The doors are wide open for those who seriously accept this task.

The Book Case, or the Local Christian Book Vendor (Colporteur)
One of the best-selling books in Britain after World War II was the story of Douglas Hyde, who joined and was active in the Communist

party until he became a Christian and left the party. I will never forget reading that, as soon as he became a party member, he was assigned to collect subscriptions in his own neighbourhood for the Communist paper, the *Daily Worker*—which was not at all an easy proposition.[45] But you could hold no membership in the Party which would not at the same time oblige you to help spread the Communist ideas through the medium of print. Most Christian churches could learn something from that.

The second step which the individual Christian can take beyond the occasional sale of a book is the work of the colporteur, properly speaking, i.e., the systematic visitation of all families of a neighbourhood with Christian literature for sale. Some have raised the question whether we should not again have full-time

---

45 D. Hyde, *I Believed. The Autobiography of a Former British Communist*, (London: Heinemann, 1951).

peddlers for Christian books like the 19th century. I understand that for the time being this has to be answered in the negative. It is doubtful whether the turnover achieved would be sufficient to cover the necessary expense.

However, there may be positive reasons which make it even seem preferable to aim at developing a larger group of honorary, unpaid, local door-to-door vendors. Of course, there are already many door-to-door campaigns where young people make themselves available for some weeks or months and take on this missionary activity in another part of the country or even abroad. However, it seems best if this work were done by someone who lives in the neighbourhood himself and is known for the distribution of Christian literature in his spare time.

Naturally, such a representative for Christian books can also cover local Christian associations which do not themselves have books on sale. More important will be the numerous outside encounters with people which often have no longer any relation to the church or the Christian message. The local Christian book representative would not only sell books but have opportunities for counselling which are no longer open to the official representatives of the church. Moreover, he or she would have the advantage of coming as a Christian and not immediately with the colours of a particular denomination.

What I am saying is that even the mere presence of the Christian book representative at the doors is an invaluable piece of witness. People see that the Christian faith is alive, and alive in their own neighbourhood. One-time drives, coming in from the outside, remain an alien element to local life. On the other hand, the neighbourhood spare-time Christian book worker stays in the block, the suburb, the satellite town, in this village or the neighbouring one.

A colporteur might use a flat case like an attaché case, if somewhat larger, which will not be too heavy, but practical for the display of books and booklets. A supply of further copies could wait in the car. He or she would even when not selling anything leave a tract or a carefully selected brochure, perhaps with his address.

Now, I believe that this courageous and engaging kind of propagation of Christian literature more than anything else deserves the support of churches and organizations, and especially of the experts—Christian publishers and booksellers. This is where the professionals of the Christian book trade should come in and take particular responsibility.

They should initiate and organize regular training weekends for these people and for all those who want to make progress in their personal commitment to literature work in the churches and in missions. Such training weekends could assist them with lectures of more basic concerns, with practical hints and mutual encouragement. What is true for the whole of industry will be especially true for a Christian enterprise: The best capital is always people. It is our task to nurture and develop them… Make people your purpose! In some countries there still exist groups of loyal church members who as it were represent a remnant of the former colporteurs: those who go around and distribute Christian magazines to subscribing families. Could they not take along a carefully selected popular book every three months and offer it for sale? Of course, an announcement and review of such books in the respective magazine would be a necessary underpinning.

Surely a magazine subscriber is the primary potential reader of Christian books. It is highly desirable that the editors of those magazines which are still personally distributed door-to-door should also especially cultivate the circle of these distributors, inviting them to weekend retreats and regional afternoon conventions so that the individual may find new inspiration and motivation through the larger horizon and the greater consciousness which can be shared at such meetings.

Occasionally the neighbourhood strategy can be replaced by providing members of a professional group with Christian literature. There is the magnificent example of those two senior ladies, widows, who at a central customs and transit point between Switzerland and Germany provide drivers of the innumerable international freight trucks with Bibles, Gospels, and Christian tracts in their respective languages. By now, Scandinavians, Russians, Romanians, East Germans, Italians, Turks, and Dutch already know the two women who according to age could be their own mothers and who—come rain or shine—are on the job between parking lot and barrier with their little cart full of Bibles. Drivers sometimes even ask for them, when they pass through again. The two ladies have since been given permission to set up a small camping trailer near the border which serves as "warehouse" and place for rest. If someone would collect these stories, of which there must be more than one, he could demonstrate how still today Christian literature work is experienced as true adventure in God's service.

The Propagation of Literature Within the Congregation: The Book Table

The book table primarily serves the propagation of Christian literature within the church.

It would be highly desirable if a book table were present at all meetings of the congregation, including Sunday morning worship. It should always be serviced by one or more members of the church. This is far preferable to the wooden bookcase still in use in some churches which stands on the side, mute as a fish, and more often than not testifies to its neglect by the congregation through the yellowed and dusty state of its printed matter. Again here: the best capital is a committed person who takes responsibility.

We suggest that in each congregation there should be a small committee for Christian literature work, just as there is the finance committee and a team looking after the premises. The work of the literature committee should also figure in the budget of the church. If it is handled wisely and with discernment, it may well soon figure in the "income" column.

Where there is not as yet provision made in the budget, the literature work can get started or be constantly supported by individual subscriptions and one or more collections taken in the congregation.

The Congregation's Literature Work in the Marketplace: The Book Stall

It is well known that congregations (and youth groups) thrive when they commit themselves to targets beyond their own circle, i.e., where they are not content with the wooing and cuddling of their existing membership. In recent years, work with Christian literature has provided an excellent means for missionary outreach, beyond the limits of the immediate congregation. It seems to be the appropriate means for the activation of the lay members or the church.

In this area there exists a large number of remarkable examples of which we can here only mention a few. One Christian youth group sells secondhand Christian books in a flea market. In some parts of Europe, young Christians have set up revolving book stands in shops, bus stations, and lobbies of hospitals. In Sweden and in North America, this method has helped to distribute hundreds of thousands of Christian paperbacks. One church in Switzerland stepped up their literature outreach during an evangelistic campaign and sold in a small town over a short period of time books worth 20,000 Swiss francs (7,000 pounds sterling at the time).

I especially enjoyed the idea of one youth group which, after careful planning, borrowed a trailer from a construction firm for the duration of the local annual fair in the autumn and furnished it as a tea-and-book mobile. Many loved to come for a hot cup of tea or coffee into the cozy trailer and browse through the extensive display of Christian books on the shelves. The turnover was such that this group has since been thinking of fitting out a book van for regular service.

The whole idea points to the next step: the establishment of a permanent tearoom with book stalls, run by the local church. One thinks, e.g., of the St. Aldate's book and coffeehouse in Oxford. A Christian student work in the United States has set up six bookshops on university campuses: a shrewd move to establish a visible and continuing Christian presence on campus. I am personally aware of at least one other congregation which recently set up such a combination. A Christian publishing house has pledged support, and a group of people from the congregation have made themselves available so as to keep the shop open during the afternoons.

The Literature Work of a Regional Association of Churches: The Bookmobile and the Book Exhibition

One may feel that in what has been said so far, we are approaching the limit of what an individual congregation can do through its volunteering members. The larger enterprise is the responsibility of a regional association of churches or a specialized missionary agency. Several churches in a city working together could arrange a highly visible Bible exhibition, plus sales drives sponsored by a Bible society. In one city, churches combined to hold a "Bible Day" with exhibition, advertising, and the free distribution of ten thousand copies of St. Mark's Gospel in streets and shopping centres.

Well-known from Italian beaches in the summer are the mobile book kiosks of the sisters of the Paulist order. In Germany, a Christian fellowship has bought a bookmobile and a market stall which move around to rural fairs and markets. They set up among the other traders' stands and sell Bibles, evangelistic literature, records, and tracts. Recently, I have seen pictures of similar stands selling Christian literature in places like Chile and a country of the Middle East.

The German fellowship mentioned lays special emphasis on the participation of a local group or congregation. One report reads: "The boys' group came for a visit, bringing their friends. The older youth and the group of young adults helped at the booth on a rotating basis. The senior members of the congregation joined us with their prayers, informed others, prepared the meals, visited the stand and helped cover expenses."

Part of a regional association's or a diocesan task would also be the arranging of training courses in the dissemination of Christian literature, as mentioned before. Bible Societies have pioneered training of distributors through the "Penzotti Institutes" developed in Latin

America. It is thought that particularly this type of work has had a large part in the speedy expansion, especially of evangelical denominations in that continent. This method has helped toward three things: 1. It has caused the churches to go into action in civil communities, 2. It has awakened the testimony of church members, and 3. It has enabled the local congregation to grow spiritually as well as in numbers.[46]

It goes without saying that all the activities mentioned should be organized in close cooperation with the local Christian bookstore or bookstores where they exist. A Christian bookstore is in fact an ongoing exhibition of Christian books and will continue as a prominent means of literature work. However, what can be said and suggested concerning a further vitalization and development of that instrument, we will leave to the advice of the experts.

---

46 Olivier Beguin, in *Christ und Buch*, (see n. 25), p. 17.

At least one thing can be said about the particular situation of and promise for the Christian bookseller (and publisher): For him or her, the ideal purpose here coincides with the material purposes without which we cannot do as human beings. A good book sold means income and spiritual advance. In this way, I consider the Christian publisher and bookseller a full-time worker for God's kingdom just as much as the preacher and pastor. If we can say of the mission-conscious Christian, as we have tried to establish: "Every Christian missionary a bookseller!," we should also claim: "Every Christian bookseller a missionary!"

Aim and Purpose of Christian Literature Work

All suggestions that have been made are of course not intended merely to incite some hollow activism. In Christian perspective, success in sales can never be an end in itself. Christian literature work is a means to an end. Whoever works or intends to work with Christian literature, indeed everyone who helps in the Christian church, must try to gain deeper insights into the purpose of his or her actions. What are our aims? What are we living for? What is the horizon of our work and commitment? Clarity of purpose has a liberating effect. Especially in a time like ours which suffers from a fundamental "crisis of meaning," it is like fresh air and fresh water when someone sees the light concerning this question.

Wherever the aims are clear, one will also be conscious of the part played by the printed word in the pursuit of those aims. Besides preaching and personal conversation, Christian literature has a prominent part in the realization of the all-encompassing purpose of Christianity at any given time: to present each living generation of humanity with the invitation to and the challenge of the Kingdom of God.

This is a far-reaching task, both in its breadth and its depth, as Paul formulated it: "in all wisdom to present every man mature in Christ; for this I toil, striving with all the energy which He mightily inspires in me" (Col. 1:28f.). Books are tools and means to this aim; their production and distribution is not an end in itself. We need to keep this in mind, both generally and in the individual situation.

Books are mighty weapons in the daily battle whether Almighty God or the imaginary "almighty man" is to rule on earth. This battle front is the true background and meaning of the history of humanity. In this war, books are carriers and communicators of ideas of the utmost importance. Not in vain do we talk of the "explosive effect" of this or that book. Books are able to carry powerful ideas into the hinterland of the spiritual enemy. Therefore, as Christians, we need to learn how to employ this medium with the highest possible efficiency.

Christian proclamation always takes place in concentric circles. As the book of Acts shows, Paul has to address pagans in Greece in a manner different from that with which he speaks to the members of the Jewish dispersion, because the heathen do not as yet have the presupposition for an understanding of the message of the Messiah. In our present time, it is particularly Francis Schaeffer who with his books has fought for the development of a "pre-evangelism" appropriate to our own cultural situation. Even in Europe's "post-Christian" era, it can happen that a university student has never heard the story of the Prodigal Son and is deeply impressed by it.

We have to take account of this situation. We need books which address the broad range of very different presuppositions of understanding in today's secular world. We need other books which will lead a person into the depth of God's plan of salvation. In this way, books are an eminently valuable tool of missions today. They help to spread the message to the multitudes of people.

A book reaches people to whom I cannot go. It can speak for me when I lack the respective language. Just as Moses had Aaron appointed as his spokesman because he felt he could not speak for himself, so many of us can use a book that will speak for us in situations when we perhaps are not skilled to speak.

Books, however, also serve the deepening of the faith. Therefore, they are essential tools for church seminars and training courses. Bible study groups and meetings gathering around a Christian book are decisive means to the consolidation of faith and doctrine.

Finally, reading is essential for nurturing one's own soul. Today we need to recover the rich tradition of Christian spirituality. Surely that will be costly and an effort for some of us who would rather watch some entertainment on T.V. Soon, though, the moment will come when we are sorry for the good opportunity that was lost.

Books are particularly suited as a means to reach individuals and isolated persons. They have always been the means of communication for Christians dispersed, sustaining them and strengthening their unity, until the little flock gained public relevance. Books are the decisive instrument of minorities. Often, they hold up the cause in the years of spiritual depression.

One might say that Christians are by definition a minority in the populace. They are either a minority which grows into an all-encompassing movement of renewal, or—at other times and in other places—a minority without that influence that would give them access to the mass media and the public mind. It is always a time for books. In this respect, the printed work remains also today an ideal tool of Christian proclamation facing a powerful spirit of secularism and godlessness: it may well again prove a sling of David for a giant doomed to destruction.

In conclusion: Working for the dissemination of Christian literature is a great task. If, according to the *Concise Oxford Dictionary*, "to publish" means "to make generally known, to noise abroad"[47] it is essential as a Christian activity. Christian book work must "go public," be daring and aggressive. Its task is not to hide but to invade.

Christian literature has a great responsibility. This is how James Freeman Clarke put it:

---

47 As quoted in *Introduction to Book Publishing*, ed. Mary Perry, (Britain: Publishers Association, 1977), p. 17.

"Let us thank God for books. When I consider what some books have done for the world, and what they are doing, how they keep up our hope, awaken new courage and faith, soothe pain, give an ideal life to those whose homes are hard and cold, bind together distant ages and foreign lands, create new worlds of beauty, bringing down truths from heaven—I give eternal blessings for this gift, and pray that we may use it aright, and abuse it not."[48] But work with books also has the highest promise. Rightly did Thomas a Kempis say 700 years ago: "If he shall not lose his reward who gives a cup of cold water to his thirsty neighbour, what will not be the reward of those who by putting good books into the hands of those neighbours, open to them the fountains of eternal life?"

---

[48] As quoted in *AB, Bookman's Weekly*, Feb. 25, 1980 (title page).

www.ingramcontent.com/pod-product-compliance
Lightning Source LLC
Chambersburg PA
CBHW052159110526
44591CB00012B/2002